Schoolyard of Broken Dreams

MARVIN TATE

TIA CHUCHA PRESS
CHICAGO

ACKNOWLEDGMENTS

Special thanx to Luis Rodriguez for having a vision like Tia Chucha Press and to Michael Warr, whose friendship and professional guidance will forever be appreciated. And to Lucy (My BaBee) for whom without her love and patience, this book would still be on the back of some fucked up azz napkin.

Shouts go out to the Tate family; James, Freddie, Linda, Pete, Melvin, Aunt Honey and Unc' Herman, C.J. Bani, Ainsworth, Leroi Bach, Uptighty, the Funky Wordsmyths, Forest, Minnie, and George, Kate and the Bop Shop Clan, Eddie Arocho, Angela Jackson, Estelle, the Muellers, Willie Ferguson, Kiki, Garfield, Tony Dawg, John Gans, Marc Smith, F.A.T.E., Cookie, P. Funk, Rohan Preston, Rev.Woodson, June Pycosack, Aleene, Yellow Sunshine, John Starrs, Annie Schultz, Room 211 at Brown School, South Lawndale and God.

peace out

Some of these poems have appeared in the journals PLANET ROC, PERMANENT PRESS, *and* HAMMERS, *and the anthology* STRAY BULLETS — A CELEBRATION OF CHICAGO SALOON POETRY. *They have also been featured on two compact discs:* A SNAKE IN THE HEART, *a compilation of poetry and music by Chicago spoken word performers, and the new* UPTIGHTY *disc.*

Cover photos: Lucy Mueller
Design: Jane Brunette Kremsreiter

Printed in the United States

ISBN 1-882688-03-1

Library of Congress Catalog Number: 94-76368

Tia Chucha Press
A Project of the Guild Complex
PO Box 476969
Chicago, IL 60647
312-252-5321
Fax: 312-252-5388

This project is partially supported by grants from the National Endowment for the Arts, the Illinois Arts Council, and the City of Chicago Department of Cultural Affairs. Special thanks to the Lannan Foundation for a grant to publicize this and other Tia Chucha Press projeccts.

To the memory of my mother and friend, Ophelia Tate.

*"I'm going to move on up a little higher
going to shake hands with my father…"*
— Mahalia Jackson

CONTENTS

ATTENTION GREEN LINE TRAIN RIDERS

EL TRAIN CLOSED FOR RECONSTRUCTION FOR TWO YEARS.

ALTERNATIVE SERVICES AVAILABLE.

A BLACKOPOLIX

*"electric lights go off, but a candle
light will see you through..."*
                    — Bobby "Blue" Bland

Inside the dark and crowded aquarium
she listens to the many voices outside
her living room window; they are crooning
gentle souls, unaware of the blackness
that has surrounded them.

inside the dark and crowded aquarium
she consoles Nita and Ben, with stories
that her mother once told her, when she
was young and afraid. Nita falls asleep quickly
while Ben, with all of his father's false
bravado, tries to stay awake until all of
the lights in the house are on again or until
the sun appears behind the thin curtains
like a horrific spotlight.

inside the dark and crowded aquarium
a candle does a quick and exotic mambo
seducing confused insects into it's tiny
torch like fingers and ice melting slowly
in the belly of the old refrigerator
searches for a place to settle inside
the cracks of the wooden floor
soon she will fall asleep too, perhaps
on the green sofa with Ben and Nita
or maybe she'll make a pallet for herself
near the open window, where she'll listen
to the dreams of strangers being robbed
by the greed of blackness.

TURN DAH FUCKIN' LIGHTS BACK ON!

Late last night
I was taking a bath
when all of a sudden all of the lights in my house
went out

I had to ask myself;
"DID YOU PAY YO' BILLS ON TIME?"
...HELL YEAH. so what in the fuck
could it be this time?
For three nights in a row
a blackopolix and not by choice
"unh, unh, I said to myself
we don't need this
I ain't no John Boy,
AND WE AIN'T THE WALTONS."

SO YO EDISON,
COMMONWEALTH EDISON,
TURN DAH FUCKIN' LIGHTS BACK ON!

I lit a candle
so I could put my clothes back on
then I walked down to what use to be
the grocery store,
I blinked my eyes
cause I couldn't believe
what I was seeing,
these crazy azz cops
knocking my people upside their heads
acting and thinking
like this was still 1968!

1968!

do you remember what Bob Marley said?
"A hungry man is like an angry mob..."
he'll cheat, steal, kill before he starves,
but tell me, honestly,
DO YOU THINK POOR PEOPLE
DIG LIVING LIKE THIS?

no compensation,
and never an explanation
so crooked politicians beware
we don't need the bullet
cause we got the ballot.

SO YO EDISON,
COMMONWEALTH EDISON
TURN DAH FUCKIN' LIGHTS BACK ON!

MRS. BROWN'S FIVE AND DIME STORE

She will never buy
from the Korean store owner
ever again
not since he ripped open
her big brown paper sack
watching the cut up Polaroids
scatter like crazed confetti
across the black and white floor

assuming that she had stolen
one of their exotically grown kiwis
or fresh succulent egg plants
she put up a good fight
cursing in her thick
Mississippian accent

she even managed to hit
the tall goofy one standing behind
the register with an Ali borrowed right
as he shook nervously with a pistol
in his hands

Mr. Wilkerson our drunken next door neighbor
and sometimes community leader blames it
on their being new to the land of good and
plenty of have-nots and that every community
should be run like a small country and that
if we can't control what goes on in our own
neighborhood then we have no one to blame
but ourselves

there is a rumor of a peaceful boycott
of the Korean store owner who argues
convincingly that he was born in the
good old U.S. of ASSUMPTIONS and that
he screams into the TV cameras, "When two
cultures live side by side and neither one
knows nothing about the other, then you're
always going to have a conflict of interest."

a crisp scent shatters the cool summer night
the picture of a smiling politician's face
is blown into the teeth of a barb wire fence
as if trying to escape another broken promise
there is talk however on both sides to try to
understand each others' differences but even
an old drunken fool like Mr. Wilkerson will
tell you that there won't be no peace until
there is trust...

A BRUISED MOON OVER
THE CABRINI GREEN PROJECTS

I am the dark and ominous tower
your greenless, infertile backyard
the unsightly vista that you view
each morning, from your high rise
curtainless, kitchenette windows.

there are no blond or red hair damsels
screaming from my broken windows,
there are no pretty freckled-face kings
sun tanning on my front lawn.

when you see me, you think SELL IT!
when you hear my name, your heart quivers,
SELL IT!

to some, I am an off the path tourist attraction
a must see, real Chicagoan jewel
I've even heard that in certain circles
wayward junkies have found my dusky den a haven
away from their sleepy side street mirages
but to you, I am the experiment that failed
the perfect excuse for you to chase away
the last store front, the last factory
the last father out of their natural setting
as you go on tearing and destroying and replacing
with plastic villa domes and soul-less restaurants
your version of a safe yuppie, buppie ghetto.

I see your invisible for sale signs
disguised as police protection,
rehabilitation, an economical migration
of pseudo liberal conquest of elimination
without assimilation.

CABRINI GREEN PROJECTS BOMBED AND SOLD
BY THE CITY OF CHICAGO: LOOK FOR MCDOME SUPER
COMPLEX COMING SOON.

SOULVILLE REVISITED

Greg Williams had changed
he had decided one day that he wasn't
going to be black no mo'
said that he was tired of seeing black

tired of eating
                                        dreaming
talking
                    walking
freaking
                        fucking
thinking
                                worrying
b l a c k

burned his 100% rayon dashiki and swapped
it for a Dead Kennedy jacket complete
with Sid and Nancy buttons and a pair of
construction orange combat boots

told me that revolution was just a bunch of
poor folks stuck in reverse, talking that
race rhetoric and that the only revolution
that he was going to be down for was getting
his glass dick back from his boy Lonnie
who was using it all last week

gone is his once bushy
                                    erratic

Jupiter
                    Sugarfoot/Hendrix shaped

afro fade and now he's digging a government
cheese colored mohawk

yeah, Greg was known for changing, sometimes
for the worse, he'd be talking like somebody

had poured some 7UP into his funk; the last
I heard, he was hanging with this phat freak
named Wanda, they were talking about flying
to Pluto to check and see if Sun Ra had any
of that space pot for sale. I told them to
give me a few dollars and I'd take them
anywhere they wanted to go
in my space shuttle...

DINNER TIME (1965)

Shadowed on the wall
in a candle-lit room
six wool-headed children
huddling around a three-legged
table supported by wooden boxes
with only grits to eat
and five spoons
like Indians we sat, hunched
with triangle closed hands
and closed eyes, praying.

GI BLUES

FOR OPHELIA

She forgot to close the bedroom door
the door that leads to her dress rehearsal
where nylon stockings snaked around the door
knob hang like old hound dawg jaws and
the radio plays a young Aretha, moaning,
"Am I Losing You?"

his picture stares deceivingly at her
from on top of the crowded dresser
he is amused at her swollen face and eyes
that can no longer hold in place
hot sticky tears, as she gets ready
fooling and believing, that after five long years,
that she still couldn't live without him

that after five long, lonely years
that whomever's hot, tight pussy
he was shaking inside of, that one day
one of those good old down south kind of days
where the sun shines like lemon skins
that he was just going to get up
and come back home, just like in the movies
in his deadly red zoot suit, fake azz
black patent shoes, beat up tilted fedora
marching home to this shit
....1....2....3....4

BLUES JOINT

When she wore that black dress
there was no telling how she was coming back
home, half drunk, half way smiling,
half way crying

when she wore that black dress
the one where the beaded strings frantically
danced every time she'd strike a different pose
on the bar stool, like a young Dorothy Dandrige
beautiful and extremely lonesome

when she wore that black dress
way above the knees before it was fashionable
she'd forget about home
work at the factory or choir practice and the gossip
among the neighbors that she was a whore
out on the prowl for their sorry drunken men

when she'd wear that black dress
the one she stayed up all night long sewing
the rip in the hem; she'd dream of the things
that made her happy
Sam Cook could make her happy
as she danced to his soulful voice
all alone in the living room, with the lights
turned down low and that black dress
dangling in her arms.

QUEEN BEE

She likes to show pictures
of herself when she was beautiful
to her grand daughter and to the nurse
who will watch over her
while she carries on conversations
with her cunt.

her favorite memory
is doing the Watusi
in her Aunt Harriet's living room
they are preparing to go somewhere
maybe to the T. Box lounge, to hear
a young Wolf, howling and crawling
underneath their table.

there are other pictures
where she is wearing the same dress
cigarette burns cover all five pictures
blotching out the years they were taken
she is enjoying herself.
"Life is too short to dwell on the past"
is what the pictures would read
if they had voices.
The granddaughter can hardly believe
that her grandmother was once beautiful
she sees herself and her mother in the
old woman's eyes and begins to cry
wondering if she too, will live to die
this beautiful.

ODE TO JOHN LENNON

So you want a revolution?
hello john, I watched you
on the ten, eleven and twelve
o'clock news last night

thanks to you john, they're
talking about stricter
hand gun control, very heroic
john, but my son died yesterday too
in a cross fire, nothing new
john, the black ghetto and its forever
growing problems

half the world went into labor
as we sat nostalgically listening
to "Imagine" and collecting any Fab
Four material we could get our
hands on: THE GREATEST HITS OF
JOHN LENNON, JOHN'S HIDDEN SKETCH
BOOK, THE BEATLE YEARS—1964-1971,
JOHN SINGS WHILE YOKO LISTENS, ETC.

the media lauded your death
while your worshippers drowned
themselves in morbidness
at your grave site
I was not there
I am a Bob Marley, Howlin' Wolf,
Big Mama Thornton, Sun Ra, David Ruffin,
Charlie Mingus, Eddie Hazel fan;
although, at times I wonder
if naming my son John instead of Freddie
would have made a difference...
what do you think john?

OVER CROWDED

Roaches in the front

rats in the back

a stingy mother

and four lazy brothers

like a traffic jaMMMMMMMMMMMM.

THE EBONY MANNEQUIN
IN THE MARSHALL FIELDS STATE
STREET STORE WINDOW

To remain anonymous
her bent fedora tilted slightly
over her right eye

embarrassed? perhaps,
you know most nude women are
when strangers stop and stare

I noticed how she reached
sadly towards me, as if I were her knight
in black jeans and beat up cowboy boots
to rescue her away from the glazed-eyed
audience, but I too stared

at the paint peeling from her nipples
as the window displayer hurriedly
undressed her from winter to spring fashions.

TREE

You played the silent role,
in this crime you were
like the strong man in a 1940's
gangster flick, all muscle
and no brain
but you too could be beautiful
in the spring or in the summer
hovering over a naked couple
or a quarrelsome family picnic
with your big burly body twisted
like mahogany licorice

you must've felt his limp body
dangling from your skinny arthritic
fingers, your rope-like umbilical cord
straining to hold his snapped neck
in place

unlike the trees in the land of OZ
you did not talk back, you did not
mind them patting your thick torso
instead you just stood there, old and
emotionless, your leaves yellow and red
make you appear picturesque
as they surrounded the crying mother
kneeling in the shadows of your many arms

and you are still standing tall
protected, unaccused with only
a heart carved in your belly...

THE FAMILY HEIRLOOM

You've asked yourself
if it really matters
what she wears is completely
her own decision, after all you never were
a hard core animal rights activist anyway
but then you remember watching
60 Minutes, how the producer's
vivid imagination made the mink
drip blood and how the leggy model
walked indifferently down the runway
while the beautiful buyers ooed and awed
with their cameras winking and blinking
like the time display you never fixed
on your VCR, but she is far from being rich
this I know for sure, that she will not snub you
or ill you with empty stories about the wealth
of an ex-lover or late-husband
she only has two coats, one for the fall
and this luxurious fur for the winter
so please do not scorn her, for she is
a decent woman, who has worked all her years
so that others could wake to a clean house
with cooked meals upon their tables
she is our mother and our grandmother
let her breath life, for she is a queen
who has walked down hot Mississippi dirt roads
without shoes and when she is done
taking her afternoon stroll down Michigan Avenue
let there be angels that await her to warm her tired feet.

26TH AND CALIFORNIA AVE.

Held hostage in a nightmare
surrounded by debris
without a broom
barking flunkies with iron taunt him
they do not know that he is innocent

afraid, the television watches over
him...yesterday he was threatened
by a one-eyed monster
it wanted food and light conversation
but he gave it neither

night and day death hunts him
sanity has stiffed him, he is the
bad/good guy in an endless dramadie

I never believed that he could end
up here, forgotten by a hard-core
world and me, his alter ego.

BUTTOPOLIX

She got more junk
in her trunk than a '57 Ford
wish that I had a woman like her
walking like she owns this town.

LIL' LARRY'S WORLD

I try not to make eye contact with him
he knows that my stay is short, that my
street smarts have been tampered with
by working too many meaningless day time jobs
or perhaps a woman friend who cares too much.
He wonders what's the nature
of my crime, my reason for being here,
if it can be measured up to the time
that he has served and will serve.
In another cell, someone is breaking down
too tired of trying to out psych all the others
who are trying to stay awake.
An angel tells me during a break
that the County has better facilities
with enough room to take a decent shit.

my conversation is short,
I call the dump where Lulu is staying, she is worried
but safe and will move out come checkout time
to a Motel Six; instantly I feel better.

The blood in my head is flowing again
our break is brief, back in the badly
painted cave are men who think that God
is their bailsman, their ticket out
that he will take care of everything.

There is a page that I tore
out the yellow pages,
it is a list of motels.
I imagine the hot water
running over my face, feet and hands
and the clerk sitting behind the front desk,
asking me incessantly,
"Will that be a double or single sir?
One or two nights sir...?"
My stay will be short,
is how I will respond.

HIP HOP POET

Give us a poem that celebrates

struggles

that cuts like a revolution that won

that would sing at the top of its lungs

FREE AT LAST, FREE AT LAST, THANK GOD

ALMIGHTY, WE CAN NOW SEE THROUGH ALL THIS

BULLSHIT!

sample it, in a rubba dub style, with Fela

leading the way, blowing humancentric
imagery out of his sax, THIRD WORLD LOVE !
oppressed people are going to be heard, don't
care if the 21st century is prerecorded
to look like, Europe, Simi Valley, Rush St.,
or the intersection at Milwaukee and Damen Avenues

spitting out words of wisdom
like flying knives
answers and questions will be heard
during the wine and cheese segment
of the program

rescue Jesse, drag him out from behind that
window with dirty knobs, cuz he will never
be effective sitting down

redefine blackness, the way Miles, Hendrix,
Baraka, Angela and P-Funk did; don't become
frozen in time with negritudeness,
"I've known rivers. I've known rivers, like a pick
stuck in a whacked azz afro poem..."

acknowledge the world and its many colors
and you will be immeasurable Hip Hop baby
in due time you will be dug by all, saying shit like,
"You know, he's a genius."

avant gardists will be forced to put down
their guards 'bout what is art and what ain't art,
mono-ethnic acting snobs...

while you return back to the hood

you, with your three foot nappy fade

and multi-colored juju beads

you like an inner city buzz word now

      a breath of fresh air

a Hip Hop baby, a real family man.

CHARLIE OF WASHINGTON SQUARE

I must of seen him
do that same bad azz nigga routine
a thousand and one times
tell a few jokes, criss cross his eyes
all silly, contort his face and then
threaten to pull down his pants
and take a mean stankin' azz shit
if the crowd didn't applaud loud enough
or shout, CHARLIE, yo CHARLIE...

only then would he grab his beat up Kango
sorting out the coins from the dollar bills
suspiciously looking over his back, for
beggars or even worse, crack dealers, that grew like
exotic plants on every street corner
yo CHARLIE, CHARLIE, CHARLIE...

word was out that Charlie was trying
his best to kick it; he had hooked up with
some good folks down from the N/A Center
little grey-haired lady told Charlie,
"son, if you tried hard enough, you could
learn to dream again."
no more late night rendezvous with that
two-faced white bitch, down in run down
rodent infested hotels like the St. James
with her, always leaving Charlie spastically
pacing in circles up under the arch
Charlie would be on all fours, barking
like he was some kind of mad dawg

"Yo Charlie, I got it, you know it's good
and I got plenty of it...yo CHARLIE!"

word was out around the square, that
Charlie was kicking it, cold turkey
and that whomever had stolen his skinny
skeleton from his old beat up body, could
keep it, cuz he didn't need it no more
he told me that he was learning to dream again.

MOOD SWINGS

FOR MILES

When you cleared your throat
and decided that there were other worlds
worth conquering; everybody and their mama
was writing odes about you, how you put the azz
in jazz, about how you could stare down a bull
without ever thinking twice about if you were
in the wrong space at the wrong time.

I tried that once, not with a bull, but with a skirt
you know, your infamous stare, for about two straight
years, until this skirt got wise and asked me if I was
a poet, man, I started cracking like a baby grand piano
cuz you know, I was freaking that somebody was digging
my words...

she caught me off guard, I mean, here I was with no cash
my belly was snoring and I had just got fired from another
9 to 5 trip. I was trying to brood her off by looking
all expressionless, but this skirt wasn't going out like
that and offered to buy me a steak and potato deal
from Woolworths and I've been smiling ever since.

people are weird like that, they remember you only
if they want something from you; that ever happen to you
Miles? One day, I was just hanging with some old homies
and we were talking about your brooding, found out that
I wasn't the only one trying to cop your groove.
Black Fred who had been trying it for years and ended up
with a hernia and a divorce said that if it hadn't
been for good pot and this young freak he was digging on
that he'd be knee deep in sessions.

the only person I knew, that could out brood you Miles
was my mama, man, ma could find shit wrong on a perfect
sunny day and not say a word until night fall
she was born that way; holding down the fort, while pop's
sorry azz would disappear into a bottle of whatever he
could find, leaving her, with six crazed kids. I'm sure
there were times she wanted to walk away from it all, but
I guess she really thought it was more important to keep
us together as a family; instead of chasing
that sorry azz husband.

Miles, could it be that we all might be brooders?
imagine that, a nation of brooders. Wish I could play
something for you man; while you decide on whether or not
heaven is better than hell. check it out. is Dinah as
pretty as Sarah? did Bird finally get off that smack?
does God sit in on yo' jammies?

WHEN A BLACK POET READS POETRY TO A 98% WHITE AUDIENCE

"Makes you want to holler
throw up both hands," but your mind wanders
off the page into an audience
divided into three groups:

1. mousey faced art students believing
   that Jack Kerouac-off is still alive and well
   and will be showing up later to read
   some real urban tales

2. a table full of beautiful lesbians visiting
   from Montana, with so much clothing on, that
   you start to wonder about that homeless family
   living under lower Wacker Drive

3. thrill seeking North Shore types
   who've mistaken the place for an after
   the Bears hangout, guzzling down beers
   in turtleneck sweaters

Pssssssssssssssssssssss, it's your subconscious
fucking with you, Pssssssssssssssssssssssssss
"WHAT IN THE HELL ARE YOU HERE FOR?"
that's when you jump into one of your Last Poets grooves
thinking, "this shit went over big with the brothers from
Omega last week, KILL WHITEY, WHITEY DID IT."

> "WENT TO THE MOON AND FUCKED AN ALIEN
> WHITEY WHITEY
> WHITEY!"

Pssssssssssssssssss, it's, Pssssssssssssssssssssssss

your subconscious again, it's getting the best of you
but you can't control it, to save your life...
"that's it, keep 'em scared my brother, they like it like
that, real haaarrrd and funky, that's it brother, make 'em

shit jimmy crow shit in their minds, make 'em scream
make 'em scream my brother, TAKE THAT SHIT BACK
    TO THE GHETTO
and LEAVE OUR DAUGHTERS AND SONS ALONE,
    WE CAN'T TAKE IT ANY
LONGER....

Pssssssssssssssssssssss, I think you got their attention
some anyhow, you see, the sister drinking with the loud mouth Asian
didn't get it, the art we arty than hell types ain't
going to get it because it's a "gender thang and racial paranoia
is just a civil lite thang of the past."

and when you finally open your eyes the entire audience
has turned into a long line of bungalows, circa Bridgeport 1993.

and you have your doubts too, and they start to shout "ASAHUM-
MALAKA," anybody check out those L.A. Lakers? hey my brother,
can you pour me some more of that Folgers?

Pssssssssssssssssss, they're clapping as if a conductor
is pointing at them and a few are even scared
Pssssssssssssssssss, my brother, do you think white folks
spend as much time thinking about black folks
as black folks do thinking about them?
Pssssssssssssssssssssss, my brother did you know
that "funk" used to be a bad word?

WHEN YOU HEAR THE WORD GHETTO

The first and last thought that comes strutting
through your mind are Hershey bars melting away
in the hot summer sun

a pregnant woman, who ain't really expecting
she's just obese, with k.f.c. in one hand
and loud mouth Hershey crying in the other

welfare kings and queens joining hands
and having royal arguments, just like Charles and
his old lady Diane use to do, ain't nothing
but a geographical thang, dig?

a Hershey found dead in the hallways of the
Cabrini Green Projects, where the grass is
always gonna be greener on the Gold Coast side
teenage Hersheys with cellular phones pressed
against their ears, walking like penguins and ghetto
Cinderellas setting it out in tight azz jeans
and penciled-heeled pumps that attract
brutish saliva dripping snow wolves

when you hear the word ghetto, you think of
Compton, Englewood, So. Lawndale, E. St. Louis,
Fat Albert and the gang, good timing in
the backyard with Uncle Ben grilling the ribs and
Harlem, where Langston's be bop sh Boom!
is still ricocheting off the walls of pool halls
straight into the side pocket of the preacher man,
who preaches all day Sunday
until the chicken is done

you think of long pink and orange suede
cadillacs slurping up gas the way D.D. Jackson's
old man be speed drinking his way through
another six pack of Old Gold

you think of hungry politicians that pick
pocket our minds the way Daley did at election time
Bird blowing notes harder than Air Jordan's
funk o' dunk shots and unemployment lines
curvaceously shaped like Vanessa William's azz

you think of Oprah acting out black fantasies
while living in places where their ain't no
black men; you think of Jesse pushing you
right into hell, use to be's and could've beens that
pollute the streets with propaganda of fatherless homes,
shoe shine hustlers and street philosophers that major in
streetology, the key to their survival

when you hear the word ghetto, you say to yourself,
"THANK GOD, I AIN'T LIVING IN THAT HELLHOLE..."
but what you cannot see is that the mind is a ghetto
and you are living in it.

BIOLOGY 101

Mr. Regoni is dosing off
like he always does about this time
during seventh period
counting the same empty chairs
it puzzles him; why on earth
would anybody be interested in
biology, a subject, he too failed
as a high school senior
and anyway, he could never stand
the stench of a frog, lying on
its back, belly split open

just two more semesters and its off
to the Keys he goes; listening to
Buffett sing the same song over and
over, "wasted away in Margaritaville".
sipping on fuzzy navels and deep sea
fishing, taking pictures of his wife
Deloris, snapping pictures of poor
Bahamians ...twenty-two minutes into
the day and a fight breaks out, he wishes
that they both would simply pull out a gun
and end it; who's bright idea was it to
put jealous spics in the same class room
with angry niggas anyway, he wonders
while lacing the eyelets in his shoes
warning them, that neither one will
graduate if they continue
disrupting his class

he knows that this type of third grade
psychology won't work, that perhaps he'd
done better taking his old man's advice
and studied medicine or managed the
family store, thirty years ago and so what
if dumb fucks, like Mr.Olsen,
the gym teacher, called him a "pussy"
and drop outs like Avery Cole
bragged about how
he once stole the hub caps off his '88 Ford,
wasn't it he who won the "best teacher of
the year award," 1978-1981?

jealousy and anger, they could keep it
he grins while separating the two manchilds
tomorrow he'll be humming Buffett tunes
and reading Hemmingway novels
under a fake Havana moon,
90 miles away from Cuba.

A SCHOOL YARD OF BROKEN DREAMS

They thought that the ball
would never stop bouncing,
stomping and jumping on the hot
grey gravel, like giant gladiators
ready for war

in beat up All Stars and stolen Nikes
gliding magically in the air, as if
a modern ballet, set to urban funk

they were legends, but in their own
minds, there was Packin' Pete, Bustin' Billie,
Hooker Joe, Pockets, my home boy Sweet "T,"
and there was K-Town Karen, she was the only
girl that I'd ever seen do a 360 degree,
in yo' face, yo' mama do the nasty all night long
SLAM DUNK.

someone should've told them that there would
always be alternatives, that the cheering crowd
and cute azz, smooth-bottomed pom pom girls
were not life-long contracts
and that the yellowed newspaper clippings of their once
upon a time boyish and girlish grins
inside bermuda shorts, accepting store-bought trophies
was not meant to last forever.

that the ex-loud mouth coach,
English teacher by day, co-owner of his old
man's restaurant by night, had alternatives.
No, the ball will never keep bouncing forever.

MY LIFE (1959 TO THE PRESENT)

I am a sometimes poet
a genius but in a useless
kind of way
who thinks
and I drink and I bullshit
I bullshit a lot
I am a junkie waiting for
popular culture to hit rock bottom
I am not to be confused
with a role model
I will not be your role model
I am the homeless
a CTA comedian without
bus fare
I am the youngest of five playing the role
of the worried mother and the absent father
I'm in love again but with a pushy bottom
I am an azz lover
a tit lover
a leg lover
a man's man
a woman's man often feeling broke
sucked, suckered and dry
I am a popular nobody
a pot head
a 1990's sex head
I am a serial masturbator
I'd like to give you some head
I learned to sing the blues at age four
                unemployed
                        laid off
walked off
hired and fired
I remember 1969
 the nigga with the silver gun
that shot Ophelia and hearing Fahey Flynn
report it on the ten o'clock news
"Mother of six shot 3 times in critical condition
at Cook County Hospital."

I am Marley's soul rebel
always running IN and OUT of other's lives
talking about the mind, the MIND THIS, the MIND THAT
the MIND, the MIND, the MIND, is a terrible thang
                    to fuck up
I am a creep, a tight black jean wearing faggot,
a leader without any followers
I am the original lonely playboy
campus clown, 1978-1981

          I WILL CHEAT YOU!
but I'm a honest looser
I dig Bird, Billie, Baldwin, Bootsy, Baraka,
That's My Mama, Blacula, Bowie, Monk, Huey,
J.B., Curtis Mayfield, Pryor, Chaka, Aretha,
Bad Brains, Nina Simone, Sly, Prince,
and the Hues Corporation
I am a Mister know it all
who hasn't been asked
the riqht question

tonight, I feel like a mamaless boy
tonight, I feel like a papaless boy
I confess, I CUNTFESS, THIS IS A FUCKED UP POEM
I'M Fucked UP for living it and all of you
are FUCKED UP for listening to it...
I came in last place in a big dick contest
I am the ugly duckling that married the horny whore
I am a cold bastard
a dumb bastard
a super stud
 a super pussy with a super hard on
an immature misfit
misunderstood
misinterpreted
mischievous snotty nose brat
a rib eating
                    steak eating

          okra eating

cunt eating snob

I am an UP Town freak

a Mid Town freak

a New Town freak
a freak's freak
I am an AFREAKEAN
you have nothing to fear

I am the king
but I've felt like a court jester
a queen
an ace of spade
I am a real card for people who feel sorry for me
I am an inspiration
a stargazer waiting for Sun Ra to make a cameo
on the Star Trek Enterprise
I am the bad/good guy in this endless sitcom
that you call LIFE
I am a self-denying buppie
a yes man
a back-seat man
a skin head, baptized with spit
I am a six foot, one hundred and eighty-nine pound
adonis, who cried after watching the movie,
Imitation Of Life, for the seventh straight time
I am a Jesus head
sent to jail on d.o.c. assault and battery
and possession of zig zags
I am a human time bomb
procrastinating, to die.

I HEAR

The man down stairs knocking
the hell out of his beautiful but stupid wife
again I hear the pounding of tight fists
bursting in and out of delicate flesh
and the breaking of little brittle bones
her beautiful body moving rhythmically
as if an out of control waltz
accompanied by his thrusting fists
IN and OUT, OUT and IN.

night time falls
they are talking again
I hear them fucking
he is begging for her
to forgive him but her beautiful body
refuses his pleas
again I hear screaming,
I hear silence, I hear him asking her
"Why baby, whyyyyyyyyy?"
I hear her rinsing away the blood
from her hands, again I hear silence.

PUNK

Paralyzed moments of you and I
linger in the back of my brain
like the time I told you
how I got syphilis so that you
wouldn't move back to California
from Jupiter, Illinois, or the time
I ripped the alligator off of your
favorite black shirt that matched
your shiny black eyes and burgundy
hair, after we argued over who invented
rock and roll; you called me a psycho
I knew then that we could make it
through any storm, together.

THE MAYOR OF CLARK STREET

FOR BOBBY D.

At first sight you want to believe
that its still him and not some head
trippin', fawnky reincarnated
PRETENTIOUS AFROCENTRIC DREAD
LOCKED WIG WEARIN APPARITION
prancin' and hammerin' it up
for the gullible and shockable
tourist, with his know it all
RASTA MAN accent or his, WHO YAH
LOOKIN' AT, nigguh livin' off
the hood groove.

DJ Mello spins another dub
rooted in our minds the way Gregory
blows smoke from another spliff
DAH MAYOR IZ ERE, the DJ sings
with his white ragga mama holding him
up by his skinny armpits
he webs a story together
about how he survived another
heart attack, his fourth in three years
where voodoo degreed doctors
clipped his mop-headed braids
and injected him with Demerol
and codeine, this makes the junkies
in the crowd itch with curiosity.

the dance floor is buzzing again
to Shabba, everybody is getting wicked
Barbara, the blond muffin, sees what he
does not want to see, the crowd dancing
in the neon.

he tugs at his baggy pants
as if in a gun fight
and counts the many hospital bracelets
on his wrist and laughs hysterically
in the faces of the huge bouncers
who think that he is mortal.

DIET

He's got the best looking veins
that I've seen on a man in a long time
two antennas popping out of his forehead
continuing at his neck and then connecting
again on his skinny arms, like two slithering
snakes about to attack its prey
he said he got them summers ago
breaking concrete for the city and then he
grabbed his mail and closed his hotel door.

I saw him months later walking with Angela
the crack addict from Buffalo, New York,
he looked tired and out of shape and his
veins had turned into puffy track marks.
I said, "hello," they nodded their heads
while their veins disappeared slowly like
sand castles.

FOUR DAYS OF
ALMOST PERFECT LOVE

On the fourth day
we talked about the first,
second and third day of our little tryst
she wants out of her lousy ten year marriage
I want only a warm place to stay,
plenty of food to eat, cold beer to drink,
and someone vulnerable like herself to admire
my poetry and well-worn tattoos.

We've only known each other
for eighty-four hours and twenty-
three minutes and she insists on
showing me snap shots of her two children
Ricky and Lynn, "aren't they adorable little monsters,"
she smiles maternally through cracked teeth
unlike the desperate whore that I met
at the local dive.
she is persistent and asks far too many questions.
why do you wear an eye patch?
and what was it that you said that you did
for a living again?
we laugh together drunkenly
this time, I am the one who is desperate and afraid
and although I don't show it; I think that I'll miss her
drunken maternal ways, her inquisitiveness and her two
beautiful children, Ricky and little Lynn.

THE HOSTESS

She pranced like a princess
pretending not to hear the gestures.
Winking camera flashes touched her
as she camouflaged among the guests
greeted with coats and hats
wolves, tigers, foxes, bears and
alligators laid placidly on the bed
of the Master.

politely she took orders
and other requests
sipping on an unfinished martini
the soiree was over,
the guests were all gone
sprawled in an easy chair with
thighs apart, eyes shut,
she dreams of New York City
and while dirty dishes waited
to be dealt with, she danced
carelessly through Times Square.

A SUMMER POEM

Maybe if I were a song
you'd listen to me
I would sing, "Hello, I've just
got to let you know…"
in my chaotic, New Yorkish, Jamaican,
Nigerian, Chicagoan accents
I'd tell you, how I just showered
last night's smoke and finger prints
it feels good as I watch the smiling waif
wave to me, good night.
that glass of white wine
and half of a roach, really did the job
I am beat, with half shut eyes your face
appears blurred as if on a passing train
you know, you're right, this is just
another stupid poem
maybe if I were a song
you'd listen to me.

DANCETERIA (N.Y.C. 1983)

"We spent the night together
until the morning light"
                    Lime

I was there too
met some new and old friends
you were among the shadowed faces
in your punked mane and your recent
tattooed flesh.

the recycled people thought of you
as rather odd, but not I, you're still
the same; holding on to your badly
sun-burned lover's hand, while secretly
craving for mine, cinematically
punishing a bummed Virginia Slim
between your thin pursed lips, as if
you were a young Lady Day, or a bitch
like Betty, just like when we use to
kick it.

NIRVANA NIGHTS
(THE GARAGE DISCO, N.Y.C. 1983)

No, no time for changing phone numbers

epileptic bodies under rainbow lights
hot octopussys in ecstasy
high off the music
drenched with the sweet sweat
of Chaka's belly button

dancing away the demons
hoping to never awake again

that the music never stops never

"dancebabygetofffff...."

EVERYONE IS BEAUTIFUL AFTER 2 AM

She once loved a married man
who treated her with the highest
respect, he knew when to leave
and in the morning he'd tip toe
across the wooden floor into the tiny
sunlit kitchen, carefully taking the wet
towel into his hands and washing the pots
and pans, while she slept silently.

she liked that trait in a man
and once she gained his trust,
she then gave him the keys to the linen closet
and the upstairs attic, where she kept
her paints and canvasses; he then had
the freedom to come and go as he pleased
without any complications, until one day
he drank more than usual, purposely
filling the tub with Cutty Sark and
breaking her family's heirloom, a blue plate,
with a blue colored family,
kneeling in a blue pasture
with big blue sorrowful eyes.

the two drank from the tub of Cutty
and argued about his indecisiveness and bad
taste in art, she demanded that he leave
her house and return to Rena, his wife
of ten years
being alone was the least of her worries
in fact, I think she prefers it this way
sleeping late without being disturbed,
pink blankets twisted around her pierced body
watching the sunlit shadows dance on top of her
face, feet and hands.

A MAN TRIES TO STOP SMOKING
BY HANGING HIMSELF

He has tried this cheap
and easy method far too many times
in the past he failed miserably
watching the knot in the extension cord
tear slowly like the stitching
in a Frankenstein mask

with him falling hopelessly
into the waiting chair or arms of his wife
Etta, who knew of his inept attempts
to stop smoking
in the past she tried stopping him
by grabbing his skinny arms and then pleading to him
to quit his nonsense and that if he really
wanted to end his nasty habit, all he had
to do was use her gun

Etta never did care for surprises
and had made a vow to herself that if
he ever tried hanging himself again
that she'd neither cry or attend his funeral

outside the kitchen window are children
the color of ginger playing on
yesterday's rain-soaked game of hop scotch
she envies their care-free world, where the
hand-painted sun smiles on a black canvas
and where tulips blow gentle Sketches of Spain.

MINTS MADE HER SWEAT

In another room she is finishing
off her things to do list:
put money that she'll make tonight
in the bank, buy Stephen book on
the ancient cities of Africa and possibly
visit her mother's grave site on Memorial Day...

it takes him a few minutes
before he steps out of the shower
rubbing alcohol on his back and hairy ass,
there are bruises that he'll have to explain
to a wife or maybe a girl friend

on top of the cheap vibrating bed
she empties her purse
separating coins, lipstick, handcuffs
mascara and a picture of Stephen
she wonders what he thinks of her,
tracing his tiny face with her gloved fingers

the man in the next room has finished showering
in another life, he is perhaps someone important
maybe the owner of a Starbucks or the manager
of a White Hen Pantry but tonight he leaves obediently
as told, she likes it when they're importantly submissive

the mattress makes a cantankerous moan
before it kicks in for good, she marks an X
next to his name on her things to do list
it is much later than she thought; Stephen
will want to know what took her so long
to buy him cold medicine and mints.

ODE TO AN EX-SLAM QUEEN
(FROM THE GREEN MILL LOUNGE)

She, the undisputed queen
of the poetry slam, a debutante
whose psychiatrist promised
that poetry would be the vehicle
for the new her; always saving
her best for last.

she took it a bit too seriously
the applause amongst the bevy
of popular nobodies, the hearing
of her Slavic name, pronounced
incorrectly by the heavy-handed host
on the night that she would lose
horribly and embarrassingly, to a much
lesser known, sometimes poet, she swore
that it was a conspiracy, a dishonest
attempt to dethrone her
of her self-proclaimed title
"Queen Of The Poetry Slam."

engulfed by an amber light
inside a small cubicle, she talks
about childhood, the magical tree
that grew candy only for her and the
touching of her sagging breasts
by her forgotten father, and poetry.

PERFORMANCE ART

She promised a very short poem
sitting on top of a tiny stool
in polka dotted boxer shorts
tossing a bald Barbie doll in the air
while her accomplice played on an old
pipe organ, "Life," she screamed, "is so
goddamn ugly and so is fucking poetry!"

I thought this to be very amusing
and started to applaud, but the eye-
patched kid sitting in back of me
started making an awful hissing sound
in my direction, I guess, obviously
he thought otherwise

when she reappeared on the tiny stage
she brought with her, a pair of huge
scissors and she offered them to the kid
with the awful hiss and then like a guru
she sat in the middle of an all white room
in a very expensive gown; while the kid
with the awful hiss started clipping away
pieces from her gown, he then passed it
on to the other denizens and they were all
delighted by her near nakedness and started
to applaud, but when the scissors were
passed to me, she screamed,
"Life, is so goddamn ugly and so is fucking poetry!"

the lights slowly dimmed
 she disappeared only to reappear
this time she was completely naked
and in her hands she carried a tiny diary
and she said, in a very child like voice,
"Now, I'd like to recite for you a line from Bukowski's poem
'The Trouble With Spam.'"

SF SEEKING DM

To stop his bald behavior
all she has to say is red light,
red light, red light, three times
reducing him to a blue polyester suit
with a top hat and cane
but then she would be considered a bottom
that talked too much, a preconceived slave
lacking the proper etiquette of a true submissive

his style is purely psychological
bedroom voice with a touch of authority
when applicable
but when she reveals herself to me
there are gentle bruises across her slender
back and flabby but shapely ass

I give her a drag off my Salem,
she requested that, and a glass of cold water
she knows, that this is just a game, that she could
have her way with him, in spite of her disposition
eyes covered with straps of leather and candle wax
melting between her toes.

TREASURE ISLAND

In line, I stand
behind the shoulders
of a construction worker
staring at you, from a distance
not too far, we were once lovers,
you were my first, you know?
holding your hand now
is your new friend, like you
she is so soft and very, very sexy
I wonder if she kisses and gives head
the way you used to do.

you see me, I turn and act stunned
but I'm jealously smiling, really I am.
I feel like jerking the hammer out of
this mammoth's back pocket, then
hammering you into a big bloody fleshy nickel,
then selling you to a carnival
so that everyone could see how unfaithful
you really are.

the mammoth in front of me sighs
he is impatient with our brief reunion
and moves to the ten item or less line
face-to-face, I notice that you're eating low
calorie goods now, a big change, from
the time we ate cheese whiz and greasy burgers
on top of a bed in a tiny dump hotel in
Harlem...you have to go now, your lover's
slim athletic build compliments you well
the total of your yogurt, lite Fig Newtons,
slim milk, spaghetti, lettuce, carrots,
bran cereal, TV Guide, bleach, wine and
salad dressing is less than twenty dollars
we exchange goodbyes, she looks happy
with her new friend, as the caption over
my head reads empty.

THE COCK POEM

You hugged me
like a ten inch child, crying
I felt the soft sticky wetness
of your tears, doing an exotic snake dance
down my legs.

my friend Carol, said that you looked
lovely standing at the party last night
she was stunned by the enormity of your
fire helmet.

I was proud of you
before I hurried you off to the clinic
where you complained annoyingly about
your head itching and your neck burning
I felt ashamed, as you bowed
your head down between my legs
it was inevitable, I knew that one day
your uncontrollable lust would murder you
                        us.
I can no longer look at you, or hold you
in front of the mirror, or show you off
to our very special friends. I hate you.
I'm on medication now and my beautiful wife
is screaming for a divorce
...sometimes I wish I never had you.

MAKING OUT WITH SOMEBODY FAMOUS

I envy that segment
of her life, New York City
1982 to 1986
the penthouse apartment
on the upper east side
thirty six floors in the sky
so high you can see the Brooklyn Bridge
or D'agastino Delivery Boys snacking
out of customers bags.
I've seen a few of his movies
on channel nine and imagined killing him
during his infamous love scene.
ever made it with someone who is supposed to be
famous? "yeah, I wing it, once with a big shot
photographer and the second time with Maxie Rhodes
the neighborhood favorite, who got pregnant by her
abusive father."
I say this to make her feel small and for the
moment, it works; she's allowed the breeze to
separate our locked hands, saddened, she walks
hurriedly in front of me. I can see why men have
loved her, pretty mouth, hands and feet, she is
irresistible...tomorrow we'll wake up in each
others arms, she'll want to know if I still think
she is beautiful I'll mumble something
indifferent
show her the pictures that came with the purchase
of my cheap wallet and accuse her
of having once loved Portier, Belafonte, Grant, or Josephine
...it's the only way I know
how to love her
from a distance with much envy of her past.

CONEY ISLAND

She wanted me to grow inside her
said that it was the only way
that I would keep an erection
after drinking all night
I told her about the time a fat cop
kicked me in the groin because he
didn't like the way I grabbed my
ex-wife's tits in public.

ever tried crushed ice she smiled
no, but sometimes going out for a walk
clears my brain, I said, pouring more
gin into her empty jar.
we walked down the boardwalk drinking
cheap beer out of Styrofoam cups
chasing our shadows until we ran into
a man selling free advice
I asked him where could I find a place
to piss, he couldn't believe that I asked
him such a dumb question and put on this
mime's face to prove it.

she takes off her girdle, placing it
inside an empty crate near the bathroom
this time she won't take no for an
answer; something I don't think her old
man quite understood; a beautiful woman
like her in her forties ... I tell her
that I never met a woman who cries
after having an orgasm.
she wipes her eyes and tells me that she
never met a man who when offered free advice,
wants to know where is the nearest toilet;
we laugh, drink, then cry together.

INSOMNIA IN N.Y.C.

FOR CHRISTINA

"...the night, has a thousand dialects."
　　　— *Lady Blue*

I am happy
to have her home
again, her eyes are filled
with tired excitement
I do not ask of her, how was her night
or what stranger she has seen
she'll discuss this, after the harsh
outcries of our next door neighbor
as he watches in anguish, the TV shooting
of his favorite hero, Marshall Dillon.

And so we sit, listening
to the white noise of the ceiling fan
spinning endlessly into oblivion
the junkie mother pacing the dimly
lit hallway, in search for her imaginary
daughter and Peter, the crazy ex-con
turned artist, trying to convince the
night clerk into allowing him to paint
murals in all of the ugly lilac colored
rooms, in exchange, he shall have his
room for free.

slowly she peels herself out of her blue
sequin dress, while lying on the bed, as
if a mermaid washed ashore into the hands
of the peasant fisherman; I've prepared for
her, a tub of warm water in which she
washes away the smoke and finger prints
of faceless johns...she reenters the tiny
room, I tell her how our neighbor screamed
so loud that he stopped would be thieves
in their tracks after contemplating a
robbery; she gives a reassuring smile

and gently pulls the covers over her
beautiful body, while somewhere in the
night, the sax player fills her dreams
with noise, lots of white noise.

SMART PEOPLE

We sat around saying smart things
to each other. we felt smart.
I told Coop that I had never felt so smart
in my entire life, that's when Lulu started talking
about how dumb this all was; bass speaker farting
and everybody trying to out smart one another
for awhile, I thought she was the smartest
because she wouldn't say a word unless she was
certain that she had proof of the matter.
ray told me later that she never did anything
that was smart, that her whole thang was premeditated
conversation with lots of clever wording
almost as if she was reading from a script
but it didn't matter that much to me, because
she was cute and sometimes funny, unlike Ray, who tried
to control everything and thought that he could out-smart
everybody including God. I mean, he started boasting
about how he killed a man and got away with it
when he lived down state. like it was the coolest thing in the world
taking another human being's life.
"ever kill someone?" he asked Coop, who by now
was totally pissed and walked into the other room.
and then Lemon, Ray's ex, comes out butt naked
with nothing on but these two huge butterfly tattoos
covering her tits and she starts clawing away at Lulu,
I started freaking and broke it up, turned
out that they were doing a performance piece
on women who like to wrestle.
after that everybody started laughing
at me, that's when Lulu decided to make some smart drinks
with what the refuse in the fridge: a slice of tomato,
a diced carrot, hot sauce, some ice cubes, what was left
of the orange juice and a bottle of cherries, marked
"expires 10/92" and then after that your honor, I saw Ray
crawling on his knees into the bathroom where
he emptied a pistol into his head. I guess he knew
that nobody
was going to out smart that performance
not us anyway.

DOWN STAIRS AT MS. EVE'S CLEANERS

Inside the tiny storefront
a daughter is trying to explain
her mother's ignorance
to a black man and his white wife.
That in her homeland
the word, "nigger," is never heard
that blacks are rarely seen outside
of MTV and live entertainment.

The mother is embarrassed
by her daughter's decision
to side with the two strangers,
she wishes that her English
was better, so that she could
defend herself.

I put my head back in the window
just in time to hear the talking head
on the TV report the arrest of a priest
for showing off his cock to a Catholic
school kid.

Juan, my next door neighbor,
is knocking down my door.
I tell him to go the fuck away,
but he comes inside anyhow
he wants to talk about his cute sister
dating brothers, I tell him that he shouldn't worry
as long as he treats her like a lady
I tell him that I appreciate his being
different, that its the media that keeps
all the races apart.

"It is hot as hell," the weatherman
screams at us, we agree and put our
pocket change together to buy more beer.
the daughter is still reprimanding her mother
I wonder if she really believes
what she is saying is true
or is she just taking care of business.

SAN FRANCISCO SKY

We were told by the neo-waspafarians
hanging out on Haight Street
that we shouldn't look in the mirror.
J.T., the eccentric brother, who lives
in a van off the Santa Monica Coast, agreed
that the sky would betray us
by turning it's self up side down with houses
and all sorts of birds, somersaulting down
the tenderloin, as if huge dice, seeking
a suitable place to land; that it would almost
be like Jesus, reprimanding us and then
whipping our backs with tiny wet wash clothes.

Lulu, never wants to believe me when we
laugh out loud like this; that when the fog
swallowing our ankles disappears that we will
return back to normal, that the rain running
from our finger tips will dry and that big
green shirt wearing monster, hiding out in our
hotel closet, will simply leave, vanish
never to return again.

There are no birds in this San Francisco sky
and Lulu ain't going for no diamonds, so from
our bedroom window, we watch as bums tip over
garbage cans the way farm boys tip over
cows in the night, "A ROACH IS IN MY NOODLES,"
I laugh. "A CHINESE IS IN MY NOODLES," she sings.

our hotel is shaking.
our hotel has got the shakes.
we close our eyes, for fear that we too
will fall into this huge black hole
where pink stars lip out of synch reggae,
mild-mannered punks and rappers indulge
in candle light circle jerks and where a
naked azz Carolyn Jones does a slow Watusi
to Roland Kirk's "Volunteered Slavery."

"there are too many poets in this town
and not enough poetry," Lulu whispers in my ear.
our hotel has stopped its terrible trembling,
the mirrors are all broken now I tell my girl
Lulu, that we may never get to know the truth
about Jimi ever black topping Janis, or if the
Mission district really does have the best
ethnic food in town, because we are glampires
and glampires can never bare the truth.

MARCHING IN THE MIST

When the smoke has cleared
and all the bad guys have untied
their BMWS and Volvos from their hitching posts
to drive back into the hills
of Simi Valley to greet their steamy
horny housewives who await their arrivals
like submissive June Lockharts after another
night of wife swapping in the game room

when PBS (Public Bull Shit) ten years
from now, broadcasts to the viewing audience
another flashback of a King being beaten
while peaceful protesters sit in cracker
owned dives where there ain't no bread
being broken

when the helicopters hovering
over another Crip, dripping blood
because of a crack deal gone bad
explodes like an over fed vulture
who's eaten too many niggas in it's day
burns along side of Mr. and Mrs. Chin's
wig shop, that could always duplicate
the afro that Rodney Allen Rippy wore
but will never manage the makings of Marley's
natty dreadlocks

                    will you be ready?

or will you waste time arguing
if God's chosen people are from Englewood
or Winnetka while your smoldering house
crumbles like an etch-a-sketch drawing
with invisible Century 21 signs in your
front lawn, another archaeological dig
without you there to correct his story

                    will you be ready?

when the bad guys ride off into the sunset
of another fake azz Hollywood Hills backdrop
taking with them all the money and all the jobs
only to return to see if Nicholson got front
row seats with other whacked out popular
nobodies, who all secretly dream, they all
secretly dream, "O HOW I WISH I WERE AN OSCAR
NOMINEE, SO THAT EVERYONE WOULD KNOW WHO IN THE
FUCK, I AM..."

        will you be ready?

the bad guys are all gone now
but they can still smell Watts
they can still smell Detroit,
they can still smell Chicago and Washington Heights
burning through their pig snouts and pig dreams
they are just waiting for the smoke to clear
from their eyes...

        let us all be ready!

MARVIN TATE was born December 27, 1959.
He is a Chicago native, orignally from the South Lawndale
community. An artist and founder of the spoken-word
band D'Settlement, Tate presently teaches poetry
in the Chicago public schools.